Arduino

The Ultimate Guide to Arduino for Beginners Including Arduino Basics, Tips & Tricks, Projects, and More!

Table Of Contents

Introduction

I want to thank you and congratulate you for downloading the book Arduino: The Ultimate Guide to Arduino for Beginners Including Arduino Basics, Tips & Tricks, Projects, and More! This book contains proven steps and strategies on how to become a truly gifted Arduino enthusiast. The great thing about Arduino is the flexibility of projects that can be completed. Once you have tried a few projects, consider some unique ideas of your own! This guide will give you all the basic information you need to know about Arduino, and help you to create some fun projects!

Here is an inescapable fact: you will need a basic understanding of Arduino and its processes to explore your electronic interests. Arduino is the glue that holds your electronic projects together, regardless of the simplicity or complexity of the project. As you begin to explore your interests more and more, you will truly see the usefulness of understanding Arduino. It is an affordable, simple way to link together your electronics projects.

Arduino can be used to create any number of projects-everything from a booze-dispenser to a door lock that only responds to a specific knocking pattern. First, however, you must understand the basics of Arduino.

In this book, we will discuss what an Arduino is. Then, we will discuss the main components of an Arduino board and a few of the types available. This will be followed by a discussion of some basic Arduino commands. Then comes the fun part-the projects! First, I will detail how you can build your own basic Arduino breadboard, before discussing several other fun projects that you can complete.

Now, it is time for you to become an amazing creator of electrical ideas using the Arduino board. As you read, don't be afraid to explore your thoughts! While these projects are fun, do not limit yourself. Because once you understand the Arduino board and its basic functions, you will never be limited to the electronic projects that you can complete again. If you can think it, you can build it with Arduino.

Chapter 1:
What is Arduino?

Arduino is one type of open-source platform that may be used to build electronic projects. There are two separate components that make up an Arduino platform. The first component is a microcontroller, or programmable circuit board that makes up the hardware of the platform. The second component is an Integrated Development Environment (IDE). An IDE is software that runs on your computer. It writes and uploads codes to the microcontroller.

Open source platforms are often used for those interested in do-it-yourself electronic projects. This can include building anything from a swimming robotic snake (we will be discussing this specific project in Chapter 6) to a coffee pot that sends out a Tweet every time it is finished brewing. The range of projects you can complete using an Arduino board is endless. In this book, you will find the instructions to several different Arduino projects. Some of these are simpler, while others are more complex. If you become confused, you will be able to find the schematics and codes for many of these projects online.

Why You Should Choose Arduino

Arduino has gathered quite a large following of electronics novices and enthusiasts alike. It is considered to be the optimal microcontroller for projects for many reasons:

- In comparison to other microcontroller platforms, the Arduino board is inexpensive. You can purchase very inexpensive versions that must be assembled by hand, but even the boards that come assembled are under $50.

- The programming environment is simple, which makes it very easy to use if you are just beginning to work with Arduino. However, while the platform is simple, it is also flexible. This means those that are more advanced can also use it effectively in complex projects.

- Most microcontrollers are only compatible with Windows. Arduino, on the other hand, is compatible Windows in addition to Linux and Macintosh OSX.

- Arduino offers extensible software, and is also open source. This means that the programming is simple to understand for beginners, but C++ language is also available through language libraries to allow it to be used by experienced programmers. You also have the option of using AVR-C coding.

- Arduino also features extensible hardware. Hardware is published using a Creative Commons license. This gives experienced circuit designers the privilege of making improved or extended versions of the Arduino board as long as they publish their model under the same license.

Chapter 2:
Main Components of the Arduino Board

Arduino offers many different types of microcontrollers, each suited for use with your specific project. Be that as it may, there are several components found in the majority of Arduino boards. Once you understand these separate pieces, you can begin to learn how they function together. This will give you the basic understanding of the microcontroller that is needed to begin your next Arduino project.

Power

A fundamental part of any electronics project is power. Arduino boards often feature a USB plug and a barrel jack. This gives you the option of either powering the microcontroller using a USB cord plugged into your computer or powering the Arduino from a wall power supply that leads into the barrel jack. The USB cable also serves the function of loading code onto the microcontroller. This will allow you to program your Arduino for your project.

When considering the power supply needed for your Arduino project, consider the voltage of your power source. The majority of Arduino boards only require a voltage of 6-12 Volts to function properly. Using a power supply over 20 Volts is likely to destroy your board.

Voltage Regulator

The voltage regulator is like a gatekeeper for the power supply of your Arduino. In the event of a sudden surge of Volts that may harm your microcontroller, the voltage regulator will turn away the extra Volts. Remember though, this does not guarantee your board will be protected in the event that you connect the Arduino to a power supply greater than its 20 Volt limit.

Reset Button

The reset button, as with most electronic devices, will reset the coding in the Arduino. It works by temporarily connecting the reset pin of the device to the ground, sending the message to restart the coding of the Arduino. You may find this very useful during testing, particularly if you have created a code that does not repeat itself. The reset button is also very functional in Arduino testing devices, such as the gas sensor you can learn to build in Chapter 10 of this book.

Main Integrated Circuit

The integrated circuit (IC) is a part that can vary slightly between Arduino boards. When you need to upload software to your microcontroller, you will need information on the IC that has been used. The reason for this is that the number of pins, as well as the functions of the board can vary between microcontrollers. You will learn more about the differences between some of the most common Arduino board types in Chapter 3.

Power LED Indicator

You will notice that Arduino boards have a small LED next to the word "ON" on the board. Whenever your Arduino is connected to an external power source, this LED will light up. If it does not, then it is highly likely there is a problem with your circuit. This could mean you have connected wires incorrectly (if you are working with a project) or that you have a short in the circuit board. Always be sure your Arduino is properly grounded to help avoid shorts.

Transmit Receive LEDs

The Arduino transmit and receive LEDs light up on the Arduino board, depending on whether the microcontroller is interacting with the IDE. If the microcontroller is transmitting or receiving data, then the corresponding LED will be lit. This often occurs when a new program is being uploaded to the board, or if you are sending out a signal to make a connected device perform a function.

Pins

The Arduino board features several different pins. Here are the pins you should expect to see on any Arduino model:

- Analog- Analog pins are used to read signals sent out by an analog sensor, such as a temperature sensor. This is then converted into a digital value that can be read by the human eye.

- Digital- These are located across from the analog pins. They can be used for digital input and output. Their functions include sensing when buttons are pushed and powering LEDs on the microcontroller.

- PWM- This will be represented by a tilde symbol (~) next to select digital pins on the Arduino board. PWM, or Pulse-Width Modulation, are responsible for stimulating output of analog sensors.

- Analog Reference- The analog reference pin (AREF) is one that you are not likely to work with. If you do use it, it will be to set an external reference voltage. This allows you to set a voltage between 0 and 5 Volts of power as the highest input for your analog pins.

- 5V & 3.3V- These pins are responsible for supplying either 5 Volts or 3.3 Volts of power, respectively. It is likely that the components running from your microcontroller can be powered with this amount of electricity.

- Ground- This appears as "GND" on your Arduino board. This grounds your circuit. You will notice several pins that can be used for grounding on the microcontroller.

As you read further through this book, you will learn better what each type of pin can do. The function that each pin performs, along with the code that is uploaded to the Arduino has a large role in how your board can function with the devices that are attached to it.

Sensors and Shields

While the Arduino microcontroller can perform some functions on its own, it is likely you will need to work with outside components for your projects. Some common external components of the Arduino board include sensors and shields, many of which are very compatible with the board. Sensors can help your Arduino measure pressure, acceleration, radioactivity, humidity, temperature, light, and more. Shields are circuit boards that have already been constructed to fit on a microcontroller. They can give your Arduino the ability to connect to the internet, provide wireless or cellular connection, control LCD screens, control motors, and do many other things. While sensors and shields are very common components of the Arduino board, you will find that the microcontroller is not limited to working with just these parts. As you go through the tutorials, you will see just some of the ways that Arduino can work with the components around it.

Chapter 3:
Types of Arduino Boards

Arduino manufactures several microcontroller types. You may also be able to find derivatives of Arduino boards, which are Arduino that have been modified by others to perform different tasks. There are five main types of Arduino microcontrollers, the Arduino Uno (R3), Arduino Mega (R3), Arduino Leonardo, LilyPad Arduino, and RedBoard.

Arduino Uno (R3)

The Uno is a perfect starter board. It features a power jack, USB connection, and reset button. The Uno also has 6 PWM compatible digital pins, 14 total digital input/output pins, and 6 analog inputs. Basically, the Arduino Uno contains everything it needs to support itself.

Arduino Mega (R3)

Arduino Mega is the pumped-up version of the Uno. It features a USB connection, reset button, and power jack, like the Uno. However, it contains more inputs and outputs including 54 digital input/output pins, 14 PWM compatible digital pins, and 16 analog inputs. This board is optimal for projects requiring many digital inputs or outputs.

Arduino Leonardo

The Leonardo is the first board Arduino developed that features a USB that has been built in to the microcontroller. This gives it the advantages of being cheaper and simpler when you use it in projects. Additionally, the direct relationship between the microcontroller and the USB lets it emulate a mouse, keyboard, and anything else you can find a code library for.

LilyPad Arduino

The LilyPad Arduino is designed with a flat back and large connecting pads. This is the ideal shape for it to be sewn into clothing using conductive thread. Its protective design even allows for it to be washed. The LilyPad Arduino is compatible with a separate family of sensor, power, input, and output boards for textile clothing.

RedBoard

The RedBoard is a simpler, more stable version of the Arduino Uno. It is designed to be programmed using a USB Mini-B cable from the Arduino IDE. RedBoard has the advantages of being compatible with Windows 8, using a USB/FTDI chip, and being completely flat on the backside. It can easily upload the Arduino Uno codes from the Arduino IDE.

How to Pick the Right Microcontroller for Your Project

Before you can begin to choose the right Arduino board for your specific project, there are several terms you need to be able to understand. Understanding the following terms will help you understand the specifications for your chosen project:

- **Programming Interface-** The programming interface is the way that you need to hook up your microcontroller to a computer for programming. This can usually be done through a USB jack, FTDI Cable or Basic breakout, or serial pins.

- **Input Voltage**- The input voltage is the recommended range of Volts to use with your Arduino board. While you may be able to use a higher maximum voltage than the recommended range, it is guaranteed to operate safely within the suggested range.

- **System Voltage**- This is the number of Volts that the microcontroller needs to function. This affects the Arduino's compatibility with shields and outside systems.

- **Flash Space**- The flash space is the total amount that the chip has to store your sketch within the program memory. A small amount is usually taken up by the bootloader, however, so not all of the flash space is available.

- **Clock Speed**- This is the speed the Arduino will be able to execute commands. It is also known as the operating frequency.

Once you understand these terms and how they relate to your project, you will be able to choose the best Arduino board for your needs. You will also find it useful to know the number of analog inputs, PWM compatible pins, and digital inputs that you will need for your project. The amount of these pins varies from board to board.

Chapter 4:
Sketches and Basic Arduino Commands

Before you begin to program your Arduino, you will need to understand the basic sketch of a microcontroller. A sketch is the term used to describe an Arduino program. It is the code uploaded to an Arduino board, where it then runs to allow the microcontroller to perform specific functions. Now that you know what a sketch is, you should be able to comprehend how they work with Arduino commands. The most basic commands of Arduino involve the digital and analog pins. We will discuss these in this chapter. However, remember that these are only a small amount of the commands that you can complete using the Arduino board. These commands are used in conjunction with input and output values to write codes. Arduino codes can be long and complex. Many of them are found in the Arduino library. The flexibility of the program even allows you to write your own coding in the event that you cannot find coding to make your project perform the function that you want it to.

Basic Commands

The basic Arduino commands include BareMinimum, Fade, Blink, ReadAnalogVoltage, AnalogReadSerial, and DigitalReadSerial.

BareMinimum: The least amount of coding needed to run an Arduino sketch. Two command lines are used with this. *Void setup( )* and *void loop ( )*. The setup function runs once each time the board is started and once when the board is reset. The loop function is used to allow your program to respond and change to your commands.

Fade: This command is used with an analog output to fade an LED light on your Arduino board.

Blink: The blink command will make an LED turn on and off.

ReadAnalogVoltage: This command will allow the microcontroller to read an analog input, before printing the voltage onto the serial monitor of the Arduino.

AnalogReadSerial: This command is responsible for reading a potentiometer. It can then print the state of the potentiometer to a serial monitor.

DigitalReadSerial: This command lets the Arduino read a switch. Then, the Arduino will make this visible by printing the state to a serial monitor.

Analog

The analog commands are designed to work specifically with the analog inputs and outputs on the Arduino board. These include Analog Input, AnalogInOutSerial, Calabration, AnalogWriteMega, Smoothing, and Fading.

Analog Input: This command is used with a potentiometer to cause an LED to blink on and off as needed.

AnalogInOutSerial: This command works by first reading an analog input pin. Then, AnalogInOutSerial maps the result of the input pin and uses those results to cause an LED light to either brighten or dim.

Calibration: This command is used to define expected values for an analog sensor using a minimum and maximum value.

AnalogWriteMega: This command is designed to work with the Arduino Mega microcontroller. It sequentially fades 12 separate LEDs on and off.

Smoothing: The smoothing command is used to smooth analog input readings if there are several of them.

Fading: As the command name suggests, the fading command is responsible for causing an LED to fade. It does this using a PWM pin.

Digital

The digital functions can play musical tones, control the function of LEDs, and read pushbuttons. These functions include Simple Keyboard, Tone, Tone4, Pitch Follower, Debounce, Button State Change, Button, and Blink Without Delay.

Simple Keyboard: This turns your Arduino into a musical keyboard with three keys by using a pizo speaker and force sensors.

Tone: This command is to be used in conjunction with a Piezo speaker to play a melody.

Tone4: This uses the tone command with multiple speakers to play sequential tones.

Pitch Follower: This uses an analog input and a Piezo speaker to play a certain pitch.

Debounce: This command is used to filter noise by reading a pushbutton that has been linked to your Arduino.

Button State Change: This command allows your Arduino to count the number of times a button has been pressed.

Button: The button command allows your Arduino to control an LED when an attached pushbutton is pressed.

Blink Without Delay: This command allows an LED on your board to blink without the delay function, meaning it can blink faster or remain constantly lit.

Chapter 5:
Project to Build an Arduino Board

An Arduino can very easily be built using a solderless bread board and just a few minutes of your time (once you are familiar with the process). Once you have built the board, the microcontroller can be programmed with the Arduino programming language. Then, you will be ready to use the board in your next do-it-yourself project.

What You Will Need

You only need a few inexpensive pieces to turn your solderless breadboard into an Arduino, including:

- 440 or 840 Tie Point Breadboard

- TTL-232R-3V3 USB to Serial Converter Cable

- Small Momentary Tact Switch

- 16 MHz Clock Crystal

- 1 Row Male Header Pins

- 22 AWG Wire (selection of colors)

- 1 Brown, Black, Red 10k Ohm Resistor

- 2 Red, Red, Brown 220 Ohm Resistors

- 2 22pF Capacitors

- 2 10 uF Capacitors

Step 1

Once you have gathered all of the necessary parts, you are ready to start building your Arduino breadboard. The first step is to set up power. For this particular model, a constant +5Volts of power will be provided. You will also set up a 7805 voltage regulator.

When looking at your breadboard, you will see squares with red and black + and − symbols on them. Begin by placing one 10uF capacitor here. Then you will need to add the 7805 voltage regulator to the breadboard. Be sure you are lining up the left leg of the 7805 with the power in, and the middle power up with the ground. Now you will need the second 10uF capacitor. Place this on the power rail. Finally, if you choose, include an LED status indicator on your breadboard. This is a good idea for troubleshooting. Connect the right and left power rails with a 220 resistor.

Step 2

For the second step, you will be preparing your chip. Each pin should align with a specific slot on the board. This will ensure your Arduino functions the way that you need it to.

Number on the Board	Corresponding Pin
1	Reset
2	Digital Pin 0 (RX)
3	Digital Pin 1 (TX)
4	Digital Pin 2

5	Digital Pin 3
6	Digital Pin 4
7	VCC
8	GND
9	XTAL 1
10	XTAL 2
11	Digital Pin 5
12	Digital Pin 6
13	Digital Pin 7
14	Digital Pin 8
15	Digital Pin 9 (PWM)
16	Digital Pin 10 (PWM)
17	Digital Pin 11 (PWM)
18	Digital Pin 12
19	Digital Pin 13 (LED)
20	AVCC
21	AREF
22	GND

23	Analog Input 0
24	Analog Input 1
25	Analog Input 2
26	Analog Input 3
27	Analog Input 4
28	Analog Input 5

Step 3

Once your pins are in place, add the tact switch near pin 1. This will reset your Arduino breadboard when necessary. Then, connect a small jumper wire between the bottom leg of the switch and pin 1. The next step is to connect the 10K resistor between pin row 1 and the power switch. The final thing you will need to do in this area is connect a GND wire to the top leg.

Next, connect power and GND jumpers between VCC (pin 7) and GND (pin 8). The 16 MHz clock crystal should then be added to pins 9 and 1-. Next, add the .22pF capacitors from these pins to GND. You can stop here if you choose, and add a programming chip. If you are interested in setting the breadboard up for programming, however, continue reading.

Step 4

The connections you will need for programming include the pins GND, NC, 5V, TX, RX, and NC. Connect the GND wire from the power rail to the GND pin. Add a power wire to the

5V pin. Finally, connect a wire between the TX pin and the RX pin. Your Arduino breadboard is now ready to be programmed. You can do this by using the USB – Serial Converter Cable from the list of necessary items.

Chapter 6:
How to Build a Swimming Electronic Snake

As I briefly mentioned in Chapter 1, you can build nearly any electronic device using an Arduino microcontroller, including a swimming robotic snake. In this chapter, we will discuss the materials and process needed to build your very own swimming robotic snake. When built correctly, this snake is waterproof and can be controlled using a remote controller. If this is your first attempt at an Arduino project, you may want to choose a simpler option from one of the later chapters to start with. While this section will be fun to read, you may want to attempt building the light-up, rain-sensing umbrella from Chapter 8, the biking jacket with blinking turn signals from Chapter 9, or the Arduino gas sensor from Chapter 10 first.

Electronic Items

You will need:

- Arduino Uno

- Seeeduino Mega

- 10 Servo Motors (Remember that you get what you pay for. The nylon gears in these motors may wear out quickly if you choose lower quality motors.)

- Servo Extension Wire

- Servo Motor Shield

- 2 Xbee Series 1

- Xbee Explorer

- Xbee Breakout (with 2 rows Xbee 2mm female headers and 2 rows of 10 male header pins)

- 3 6V NiMh Battery packs

Mechanical Hardware

- Urethane Sealant

- Marine Epoxy Sealant

- Marine Grease

- Nylon String

- Green Loctite

- 2" x 10" of 1/8" Thick Rubber

- 3 Strips Each of Carbon Fiber – 1/32", 1" x 12"

- 2 2.5 to 1.25" Shop Vac Vacuum Reducer

- O Rings

- 5/16" Hose Clamp

- Convoluted Hose Clamp

- 5/16" Tubing

- 5 Servo Brackets

- 5 Injection Molded Servo Hinge

- 5' x 2.5" Urethane Dust Collection Tube

- 5 Lynxmotion C-Brackets

- 5 Lynxmotion Servo Brackets

Tools

- Solder Iron + Solder

- Drill

- 3mm Drill Bit

- Small Screwdriver

- Needlenose Pliers

- Wire Strippers

- Wires

- Angle Snips

- Hack saw

- 2-56 nuts, bolts, and screws, either lock or toothed

- 4-40 nuts, bolts, and screws, either lock or toothed

Step 1

Once you have gathered all of the various tools, electronic items, and hardware, it is time to begin your project. You will start by waterproofing the 10 Servo motors. Begin by applying the silicon marine sealant around the plastic seams of the motor. You should also apply it to the bottom of the motor (where the screws are located) and around the wire insertion area. You should let this dry for a minimum of 24 hours.

Next, unscrew the round plastic that makes up the top of the motor. Slip an O-ring around the shaft after using a thin layer of marine grease on it. Then, replace the plastic top. This is also known as the servo horn.

Step 2

For this step, you will be preparing the carbon fiber for use. Cut the 12" x 1" strips into 3 separate pieces. This will result in 4" strips. If you have a dremel handy, you can round the corners so they are not jagged from cutting. Then, place the servo brackets 3 inches apart on the strips. Make markings where the bracket holes line up. Take a 3mm drill bit and drill into the carbon fiber, making holes where the markings are. You will need to do this with 7 of your 4" strips of carbon fiber.

Step 3

In this step, you will be building the frame of your robotic snake. Begin by using the screws that come with the brackets to attach the carbon fiber. Be sure you use the bolt that came with the bracket as well. Then, take the rubber and line it up with the middle section of the c-bracket. Use these as your guildeline to cut 5 pieces of rubber that are approximately 1" x 2." Draw a dot where the holes of the bracket align with the rubber. Then, poke a hole through the rubber so you can more easily insert the 2-56 screws. These should go through the black clamp, through the rubber, and through the red bracket.

Step 4

In this step, you will be mounting the Servos motors. Your Servos should come with several parts. Begin with the rectangular cube and insert it into the four holes of the motor. The flat side should face outward. Adhere the injection molded joint on five of the motors and place them in the bracket. Use the 4x40 screws and a lock nut to screw the servo into the black servo bracket.

Step 5

In this step, you will be mounting the servos bracket to the c-bracket pairs. For the red brackets, the c-bracket should be put into place underneath of the servo bracket, but above the servo horn. A screw and bearing should be used to secure it. For the black brackets, the c-bracket should be slipped over the motor. This will cover most of its body. Once you secure these, you should have s snake-like structure that makes up the body of your robotic snake.

Step 6

To complete the body of your snake, line up the servo horns with the holes of the bracket. Ensure your horn is centered before screwing them together. If the brackets and motors do not rotate freely after being secured, apply grease between the brackets. For additional security, apply Loctite to the screws once you are sure they are in the correct position.

Step 7

In this step, you will be making the circuit board for your snake. Begin by soldering the male and female headers onto the Xbee Breakout board. Insert the Xbee. Then, take the Servo motor shield and solder it into the screw terminals. Once it has been soldered together, take your wires and connect the Xbee to the Arduino. Connect the 3.3Vin pin on the Xbee to the Arduino 3.3V pin. Jump the TX pin on the Xbee to the Arduino RX pin. Connect the Xbee ground to the

Arduino ground pin. Finally, jump the power cord between the Arduino VIN pin and the 6V battery input.

Next, solder the wires from digital output pins for the number of servo motors you are using. You should take the dOUT wires from your Arduino, and then plug them into the servo cables. Screw the wires into the screw terminals. This will attach the 6V and ground from the batteries.

Step 8

Next you will need the code to make your snake swim. You can find this in the software library on the Servo Arduino library. You will need a code to generate wave locomotion using oscillation. This will create a sine wave that travels down the servos motors.

Step 9

In this step, you will create a free standing joystick controller for the snake. Begin by plugging the Xbee into the Xbee shield. Set them atop the Arduino and make 6 button inputs. These buttons should be connected to digital pins 2-7 on the Arduino. You will now upload a code from the Arduino library to take the button inputs and output them as movement in the snake.

Step 10

This is the step where you will add all of the wires to the snake. Use the wire extenders from the servo motors and extend the wires down the body of the snake. They should end just a few inches after the last bracket. If you want to, you can tape the wires to the carbon fiber so it is easier to put the carbon fiber on.

Step 11

In this step, you will attach the batteries using the 6V/GND wires so that your snake can operate. Attach one battery to each segment of carbon fiber, using two zip ties. You should also take the wire extensions from the Servo motor so that he battery power reaches the ground and Arduino at the front of the snake.

Step 12

This is the step where you add the on/off buttons. You may want to use one for the Arduino/Servos connection and one for the water pump. Be sure you turn on the snake before the pump, because running the water pump without water will cause it to dry out and burn up. Then, cut two pieces of rubber 1.75" in diameter. This should fit inside of the vacuum reducer. You should also cut two 2' long pieces of cord to help position the snake's body inside the vacuum reducer. You will need to cut a small slit for the wires in the rubber before placing it in the vacuum reducer. You will also attach the string here. You will have power and ground wires from the water pump, power and ground wires from the on/off switches, and one string running thorough both the rubber pad and the vacuum reducer. At the tail, you will only need the string on the outside to tether the snake. Next, take the 6V wire on the screw terminal and solder the on/off button to it.

Step 13

In this step, you will elongate the snake body and prepare the battery so the water pump can operate properly. Attach carbon fiber pieces that are 4" long at the head and tail ends of the snake. Solder a battery junction and the water pump together. Next, locate the wire that extends between the battery and pump. This is where you will need to solder the switch to turn your snake on and off. Use the zip ties to attach the battery to the carbon fiber next to the Arduino.

Step 14

In this step, you will be sealing the body of the snake and putting on the skin. Use caulk on either end of the vacuum reducer to cover the wires completely. Wait at least 24 hours for the caulk to dry before finishing the project. You can use hot glue to secure the wires and silica packs to absorb moisture if you choose. You should also take this opportunity to ensure the joints are moving freely. Add additional grease if necessary. Now, slip the skin over the body of the snake. Cut the tube length if necessary so that the carbon fiber fits into the end of the tube when positioned with the string. Tie the string in a knot once you have finished to prevent slippage. Finally, you need to put caps on the head and tail end of the snake using marine grease to keep water out.

Step 15

Now that the snake is fully assembled, you are ready to mount the water pump. Once mounted, the water pump should be located close to the head of the snake, but on the bottom side. It will be submerged during operation. Cut 5/16" plastic tubing to slip over the output nozzle of the pump. Then secure a hose-clamp at the joint of the tube. Use this plastic tubing to mount the pump. You can use a zip tie to secure it. If you are interested, you can even mount a GoPro on the snake.

Step 16

Now you are ready to test out your robotic water snake! Be sure to apply grease around the plastic buttons before taking it outside. Turn the snake on and place it in the water. Once you have placed the robotic snake in the water, you will be able to turn the pump on without drying it up. Use your remote controller to direct the motion of the snake.

Chapter 7:
Projects for Your Pets

This chapter will discuss two separate projects for your pets. First, we will discuss the simple processes used to create an Automatic Cat Laser. This can be used for dogs or cats interested in toy lasers, and can entertain them (and you) for hours. We will also discuss how to create an RFID pet door. This type of pet door will only open for the pet that is wearing the appropriate RFID tag. This can give your pet access to your home whenever it wants, but will keep out unwanted critters.

Items for the Automatic Cat Laser

For this project you will only need a few different things:

- Arduino Uno

- 2 Servos

- Cheap Laser Cat Toy (Round, $3 version from PetCo works well too)

- Zip ties

- Hillman Hobby Parts

Step 1

In this step, you will be preparing the laser for use. Begin by using a screwdriver to pop the laser open. Then, cut the laser so that it will be able to fit the arm of the Servo. You should also drill a hole in the center for easy mounting.

Step 2

For this step, you will be building the tilt pan using the Servo. The Hillman hobby set should have erector set pieces that can easily be used to create a tilt pan. This will also provide the mount for your laser. Once you have built the mount/tilt pan, you can connect the Servos. One will be mounted onto the erector set and the other will be mounted on the laser.

Step 3

This is the step where you will wire everything together. Begin by attaching wiring from pins 8 & 9 on the Servos to the Arduino. The laser should be attached to the 5V pin. You should also attach the laser to a 470 ohm resistor.

Step 4

In this step, you will add the coding. The coding can be found in the Arduino library for an autonomous cat toy. Once you have uploaded the code to the Arduino via the USB port, you can sit back and watch your cat have fun! However, be cautious of the items around the cat laser so that your cat does not knock into anything of importance.

Items for the RFID Pet Door

- Arduino Duemilanove

- RF Tag

- 5V RF reader module (with antenna if you do not want to make your own)

- Sharp GP2D12 Infrared Proximity Sensor

- 12V DC Power Supply

- 2 TIP 120 Darlington Transistors

- Hall-Effect Sensor

- Magnet (this needs to be strong enough to activate the Hall-Effect sensor)

- LED

- 6" x 9" Sheet of 1/8" thick Plexiglas (can be adjusted depending on the size of your pet)

- Rubber Isolation Strip

- 2 12V Electronic Cabinet Locks

- 100 Ohm Resistor

- 4 2KOhm Resistors

- Hinge

- Hookup Wire (at least 27" of wire 26AWG or thinner)

- Serrated washers, nuts, and bolts

Step 1

In the first step, you will assemble the door. You will need to attach the Plexiglas to the hinge. Then, assemble one electronic cabinet lock on either side of the door post. This prevents them from adding too much extra weight to the door. The flap should center between these locks while it is in its resting state. Secure the magnet between these two locks.

Finally, use the wire to attach the Hall Sensor to the door. This can easily be taped to the Plexiglas so that it stays in place. If you choose, you can use the rubber isolation strip to line the door so that there is no damage if your pet happens to get its tail caught.

Step 2

In this step, you will be connecting the Arduino and the RF reader. Hook up the RFID by connecting the 5V output of the Arduino and digital port 2. Once you have attached your RF reader, practice using the RFID tag to ensure it is being read properly.

Then, connect solenoids to the Arduino using the 2k resistors. These should connect digital ports 5 and 6 with the TIP120s. You should then take the ground wire of the power supply and connect it to each of the grounds within the Arduino.

Step 3

In this step, you will attach the wiring from the Hall-Effect sensor. The wiring should run from pin 4 of the Arduino to the signal pin of the Hall-Effect sensor. You should also connect the wire to the 5V pin through a 100 ohm resistor. Take the ground and connect the ground pins on the Arduino. You will also need to connect the 5V to the VCC pin. Finally, add the LED to digital pin 7 using the appropriate resistor.

Step 4

In this step, you will connect the Sharp GP2D12 to the Arduino. Connect the out-pin of this to Analog port 0. You should also connect all of the grounds to the ground pin and then the 5V to the VCC pin.

Step 5

Now that the project has been completely assembled, you need to upload the proper coding. You will be able to find coding for the RFID function in the Arduino library. Do not forget to add the value of each of your pets' tags in the code. This will ensure only your pet can enter through the door.

Chapter 8:
Building a Pressurized Light-Up Umbrella

Some people really love walking in the rain. Have you ever wished there was a way to make your experience even better? This do-it-yourself project requires a few simple items to make your umbrella respond to raindrops and light up in the rain. You can even add a code to make music if you choose.

You Will Need:

- Arduino Uno (R3)

- Umbrella

- 9V Battery

- 24 LEDs

- 8 10 Ohm Resistors

- 8 1 MOhm Resistors

- 2 4051 Multiplexers

- 8 Piezo Sensor Discs

- Electrical Tape

- Duct Tape

- Hot Glue

- Hot Glue Gun

- Wire

- Solder

Step 1

Once you have assembled all of your items, the first thing you should do is program the Arduino. You can find coding for this project online, or in the Arduino library. You can even find a code that plays musical notes as the umbrella is hit by raindrops.

Step 2

In this step, you will wire your Arduino for use with the peizos. Begin by attaching pin 16 of the 4051 chips to the 5V pin of the Arduino. Then, attach pins 6, 7, and 8 to the ground pin on the Arduino board. Next, you will attach the Analog in pin of your Arduino to pin 3 of the 4051 chips. Finish wiring the 4051 chips to the Arduino by attaching pin 9, 10, and 11 to the digital outputs of the Arduino.

One of the 4051 chips will be attached to the piezos and one will be attached to the LEDs. The piezos will need to be connected to A5 for the code, and the LEDs will need to be connected to A0. Finish wiring by connecting all of your grounds on the Arduino board.

Step 3

In this step, you will connect the sensors and the LED strings to your Arduino. The sensors should be connected using a wire that links between one of the 4501 pins, the piezo disk, and the 1 Ohm resistor. Be sure you connect this to a ground. The LED strings should link a 4501 pin to a 1 Ohm resistor, followed by 3 parallel LEDs before it connects to the ground area.

Step 4

In this step, you will be soldering everything together. Begin by soldering the 10 MOhm resistors parallel with the piezo sensors. One side of the resistor should be linked to a 4051 pin and the other should be linked to a shared ground. If the wires of your piezos are fragile, you can reinforce them using electrical tape before you begin soldering.

Next, solder the 4051 pins to the resistors paired with the LEDs. Then Solder the wire between the LEDs and resistors, as well as the LEDs themselves. Finally, solder the end of the LED string to the shared ground.

Step 5

Now, it is finally time to attach the Arduino and its parts to the umbrella. Using a hot glue gun and tape, you will easily be able to connect everything. Remember to leave a space for a 9V battery, which will be necessary to power the Arduino. Remember to take care that the piezo discs go on the same umbrella panel as their corresponding LED lights.

Step 6

For the final step, you will be making your device waterproof. All of the exposed wires should be covered with electrical tape, so interference is not caused by wires touching. You should also place your Arduino and battery in a plastic bag, to prevent it from getting wet. You are now ready to take your umbrella out and test it in the rain!

Chapter 9:
Cool Arduino Projects You Can Wear

What better way to show your Arduino project off than by wearing it into town? In this chapter, you will learn how to build a self-lacing shoe and a biking jacket with a functional turn signal on your back. With your shoe, you will be able to avoid taking the time to stop on your way out the door and lace up your high-tops. You will be able to lace your shoes with the press of a single button! If you choose to build the biking jacket, you can look cool, stay visible at night, and improve your level of safety while you are biking on the road.

Items for Your Self-Lacing Shoe:

- Arduino Duemilanove

- Hightop shoe with thick undersole and heavy padding

- Servo Motors

- Motor Shield

- Forse Sensor

- 4" by 4" Sheet Metal

- LED and Resistors

- 9V Battery Case (with a battery clip and switch built-in)

- 1/8" Braided Nylon Paracord

- Insulated Copper Wire

- Plastic ½" Cable Loops

- Plastic Zip Ties

- Hot Glue Gun

- Solder

- Screwdrivers

- A USB A to B Cable

- Computer (for loading the code onto your Arduino)

Step 1

Once your materials are assembled, you will begin preparing the laces. Please note that the items needed only include the amounts to create a single self-lacing shoe. First, cut six 18" lengths of paracord. You will not need the inner core. On one side of the shoe, add 5 zip ties to the shoe. The shell of the paracord will then go over the zip ties. Next, the plastic loops should be threaded through the other end. Save the sixth length of paracord, because you will need this later. You will then do this to the ankle strap of the high-top.

Step 2

In this step, you will be making the mount for the Servo. Use the sheet metal and trim it until it fits the back of your hightop. Sand the rough corners and edges before drilling into the four corners. Use flat bottomed screws to secure the plate on the shoe. Be sure to leave a gap between the plate and the shoe. This will be used to attach the Servos.

Step 3

In this step, you will be attaching the Motor Shield to the Arduino. This is a simple step. Follow the instructions that have come with the shield to solder the Arduino and Motor Shield together. You will do this using the header pins.

Step 4

In this step, you will attach the motors to the shoes. You can secure the motors using rubber cement first if you choose. Then, wrap the motors and tighten them until they are secure. You can trim these down once they are attached. You will mount the battery case below the motor. Be sure that the power switch faces outward.

Step 5

Now, you need to upload the code for your Arduino. Once the code has been properly loaded, you are ready to attach all the wires and solder everything together. Begin by soldering a wire between a resistor and an LED pin. Then, push this through a shoelace socket that has not been used, securing it with hot glue. Be sure to keep track of the wire that is attached to the LED. This is very important to remember.

Next, you will need to mount the Force sensor. Do this by wrapping wire around the leads before using a drop of hot glue from a hot glue gun to keep them in place, as soldering may melt the plastic. Use glue and duct tape to secure this where your heel is in the shoe. Run these wires out of the shoe and into the Arduino.

Finally, do all of the soldering. Begin with the positive wire of the LED that was run through the shoelace socket. Solder this to digital pin 2 of the Arduino. Then, solder a force sensor wire to the 5V pin of the Arduino. The other should be attached to the Analog Pin 0, as well as a resistor. From the resistor, solder the wire to the Ground. The negative LED pin should also be connected to the ground. Once you have done this, connect four inches of wire to Analog Pin 5. The final part of this step is to plug in the Servo motors.

Step 6

The final thing you will need to do is connect the laces to the Servos motor. You can use zip ties to secure the laces, and then attach each to the servo arms. Be sure that the shoes are "unlaced" when you do this. When you activate the program, the servos will turn, effectively tightening the laces of your shoe.

Items Needed for Your Turn-Signal Biking Jacket:

- LilyPad Arduino

- A Jacket

- LilyPad Power Supply

- 16 LilyPad LEDs

- FTDI Connector

- 2 Push Button Switches

- Mini USB Cable

- Digital Multimeter (with a beeping tester for continuity)

- 4-Ply Conductive Thread

- Scissors

- Needle

- Fabric Glue

- Ruler

- Chalk or Fabric Marker

- Double-Sided Tape

Step 1

The first thing you need to do is plan where the electrical components of your jacket are going to go. You also need to decide where you would like your turn signals. Making a sketch can help with this. Remember that the power supply must be close to the LilyPad; otherwise the Arduino board may reset itself frequently, or not work at all. Once you have decided where each part of the biker jacket will go, use a non-permanent fabric marker or chalk to trace the basics of your design onto the jacket. You can also use the double-sided tape to attach the pieces temporarily, so that you have an understanding of what the final design of your jacket is going to look like. As a bonus, it will make the sewing process easier.

Step 2

In this step, you will be sewing the LilyPad board and the battery pack onto the jacket. Begin by cutting the small metal leads off of the backside of the battery pack. Stabilization of the battery is important, so use glue to attach the battery before doing anything else. You could also sew it into place if you wish. Remember that the power supply is very heavy. Choose the location you are putting it in carefully.

Now, you will need three to four feet of the conductive thread. Thread this through the needle securely before beginning to sew the battery into place. You will need to make a stitch that enters the positive petal of the power supply. Loop from the back of the fabric to the front several times, going through this petal every time. You will need to do this a minimum of 5 times. Once you have finished this step, do not cut the conductive thread before continuing.

Step 3

In this step, you will be sewing the LilyPad onto the fabric, and creating the connection between your Arduino and the battery pack. Begin by sewing the positive petal of the LilyPad into the fabric several times, just as you had done with the battery pack. Once this connection is secure, sew about an inch away from the Arduino. Then tie a knot and cut the thread. Be sure to leave enough length between the knot and the end of the thread so that it does not unravel. Take the fabric glue and go over the knots, to ensure they will not come untied. After the glue has completely dried, you will be able to trim the thread so the knot isn't so apparent.

Step 4

Next, you will need to test the conductivity of your connection. You can do this using the continuity tester. First, check the resistance to be sure it is not greater than 10 Ohms. Once you have checked this, you will be able to try the power supply. Put an AAA battery inside the pack before flipping the switch to the power. You should see a red light on the power supply. If there is not one, there may be an area where your thread is connecting the positive and negative stitching. You can use the continuity tester to check for this problem. If your power supply has been connected properly, then your LilyPad should quickly blink when the switch to the power supply is turned on.

Step 5

Next, you will need to provide insulation. When you are not wearing your jacket, and it is hanging or folded, wires may touch. This can cause them to short out, ruining your jacket. To prevent this, use puffy fabric paint to cover the conductive stitching.

Step 6

Once everything is working properly and the wires have been insulated, you are ready to add the flashing LEDs of your turn signal. You will need to sew the LEDs to the petals of the LilyPad using the conductive thread. Remember after you have finished sewing that you should use fabric glue to seal everything. Additionally, make sure your threads are not touching one another. After you have sewn these in you can download a program to the LilyPad from the Arduino library that will allow you to test the signals. You should then insulate these stitches.

Step 7

In this step, you will be placing the switches. Remember that these should be in a location that will be easily accessible as you are riding your bike. A good location would be the underside of the wrist part of your jacket. Then, push the legs through the fabric. Once they are through, bend them on the inside of the jacket before sewing them into place. You will need to sew 1 leg into an input petal of the LilyPad and another into the ground. These petals need to be located directly across from each other. Do this on both sides of your jacket.

Step 8

In this step, you will be sewing indicator LEDs into your jacket. These will provide you with feedback as to which turn signal you are using. When choosing the location, be sure they will be visible as you ride your bike. The indicator LED for each arm needs to link between the positive petal of the LilyPad and the negative side of the switch you have sewed into your sleeve. As with the other sections, you should glue and trim the knots of the conductive thread once you are done sewing.

Step 9

This is the final step of your project- programming! You can choose how long your signal will turn on, whether or not you want it to blink, or even have a flashing mode that works at night. The program you need will depend on your function. You can find this online, or in the Arduino library. Once you are sure that everything is functioning properly, insulate the rest of the conductive wiring with puffy fabric paint.

*Note: This jacket is washable by hand. However, take care to remove the battery beforehand and use a gentle detergent.

How to Build an Arduino Gas Detector

A gas detector can be a very useful tool to have around the house. Additionally, the gas detector can easily be disassembled if you need your Arduino again. This gas detector is powered by USB with an LED display that will report the amount of gas in the room. The reset button is also functional, to allow you to reset the code that will sense and report the amount of gas in the room.

What You Will Need:

- Arduino Nano

- LED Display

- Gas Sensor

- USB Cable

- USB Power Plug

- Cardboard for Exterior

- Sharp Knife

- Metal Ruler

- Hot Glue Gun

Step 1

In this step, you will mount the parts of your Arduino into the external housing using a hot glue gun. You can use small pieces of cardboard for mounting supports and spacers if you do not have anything else handy. Glue the pieces securely, but be sure to keep the buttons and contact points clear of any materials. The LED display should be mounted against the cardboard, so you can cut out an area to view the display. The Arduino will be supported at the rear of the cardboard housing. Finally, the gas sensor goes on the front side, and will stick out so that it can sense gas in the air.

Step 2

In this step, you will be connecting the wires that will make your gas sensor work properly. Begin by hooking the gas sensor wires to their corresponding ports on the Arduino. You will connect the ground of the gas sensor to the ground of the Arduino board. Then, you will connect the VCC of the gas sensor to the 5V of the Arduino. Finally, connect the Analog output to the pin you would like to use. Pin A0 is a good choice, but you can connect it to another pin if you choose.

Next, the LCD pins will need to be connected to the pins of the Arduino using wiring. Begin by extending a wire between the 5V and ground wires of the microcontroller. This wire should then connect to pin 3 of the LCD screen. Then, wire the RS pin of the LCD and digital pin 12 of the Arduino together. After this, you will need to connect the Enable Pin of the LCD display to Digital Pin 11, followed by the D4 Pin of the LCD to Digital Pin 5. Finally, you will connect the D6 LCD Pin to Digital Pin 3 and the D7 LCD Pin to Digital Pin 2. Now all of the wiring should be connected to make your Arduino gas sensor work.

Step 3

In the third and final step, you will be uploading the code to the device. You can find the necessary code in the Arduino library. Simply upload this code file and then you are ready to test out your device!

Conclusion

Thank you again for downloading this book!

I hope this book was able to help you to realize the broad number of projects that you can complete using the Arduino board. Once you understand the true potential of the microcontroller when programmed correctly, you can create nearly any electronics project.

The next step you should take is to explore using the Arduino board. Do not limit yourself to the projects listed in this book. There are several projects available online that can help you realize how to complete all kinds of projects.

Finally, if you enjoyed this book, please take the time to share your thoughts and post a review on Amazon. It'd be greatly appreciated!

Thank you and good luck!

What You Will Learn

Are you interested in electronics projects, but don't know where to start? Perhaps you have heard of the Arduino board- one of the most affordable, simplest ways to make your electronic project dreams a reality. This book is designed to teach all of the basics you need to know to use the Arduino- and to give you some cool project ideas along the way! In this book, you can expect to learn:

- What the Arduino Board is

- Why the Arduino is one of the most desirable microcontrollers for do-it-yourself electronics projects

- The main components of the Arduino board

- Different basic models of the Arduino

- How to choose the right Arduino for your project

- How sketches work

- The basic commands that can be used with Arduino

- How to build your own Arduino board

- Lots of other cool projects that you can accomplish with Arduino!

Once you have read this book, there is no limit to the electronics projects you can accomplish using Arduino. Expand your mind, and think of every project you have ever wanted to accomplish but had no idea where to start. This book will give you everything you need to make these projects a reality! Get ready to realize your potential with Arduino!

www.ingramcontent.com/pod-product-compliance
Lightning Source LLC
LaVergne TN
LVHW050148060326
832904LV00003B/63